Conversations *with* Bob

Why everything's going to be okay

R O B E R T   G E N T L E

ISBN: 1482012863
ISBN-13: 978-1482012866

Library of Congress Control Number: 2013901181
CreateSpace Independent Publishing Platform
North Charleston, South Carolina

For Julie

Contents

Chapter 1   The Food Scare   1

Chapter 2   The Coal Scare   29

Chapter 3   The Horse-Manure Scare   57

Chapter 4   The End-of-Civilisation Scare   83

Life can only be understood backwards; but it must
be lived forwards.

Søren Kierkegaard (1813-1855)

CHAPTER 1
The Food Scare

The power of population is indefinitely greater than the power in the earth to produce subsistence for man.

THOMAS MALTHUS

England

~~

1798

Do you like reading the morning paper over breakfast? Then you might have seen the following headline in 2012 as you finished your cornflakes, poured a second cup of coffee, and tucked into a serious fry-up of bacon and eggs:

> Obesity Killing Three Times as Many as Malnutrition[1]

The article refers to the findings of a landmark study published in the respected medical journal, *The Lancet*. It found that with the exception of sub-Saharan Africa, eating too much is now more of a risk to one's health than eating poorly.

No big deal, you might say. You probably see enough fat people every day at the mall, on the streets, and perhaps even at the office.

Now rewind a couple of hundred years to 1798. The problem back then wasn't obesity, but malnutrition. For many poor people, not having enough to eat was a very real problem, despite the onward march of the Industrial Revolution and the huge improvement it brought—albeit off a low base—to the general well-being of the population.

Fortunately, the 1700s in Britain was a time of innovation, growth, and change. It saw the development of improved agricultural techniques, the selective breeding of livestock, the development of the steam engine, the mechanisation of the textile industry, and the building of a network of canals across the country. A great middle class was emerging, from merchants and traders to lawyers and doctors. Wealth was no longer something you inherited; you could earn it too, no matter how humble your origins.

There was a general wave of optimism in scholarly circles. The thinkers of the day even started to envision a time when all of society's problems would eventually be solved. But then the Reverend Thomas Malthus turned up and promptly spoiled the party.

Malthus was a scholar influential in political economy and demography. As the century was drawing to a close, in 1798, he published a seminal work, *An Essay on the Principle of Population*. It would set a new tone in intellectual circles, and shape both scholarly and public opinion for generations.

Malthus believed that all was not rosy, and that the dangers of population growth would stop the march toward a utopian society dead in its tracks. His argument could be captured in this single sentence:

> The power of population is indefinitely greater than the power in the earth to produce subsistence for man.[2]

As an Anglican clergyman, he saw this situation as divinely imposed in order to teach virtuous behaviour. The poor are always with us, he argued. Their condition can never be permanently improved on any significant scale. There just isn't enough food to feed them all, so famine and wars will have to keep their numbers in check:

> The power of population is so superior to the power of the earth to produce subsistence for man, that premature death must in some shape or other visit the human race. The vices of mankind are active and able ministers of depopulation. They

are the precursors in the great army of destruction, and often finish the dreadful work themselves.[3]

Malthus's solutions were radical, though not necessarily by the standards of the time. He argued that there were two kinds of checks to hold population within the limits of available resources: positive checks, which raise the death rate (e.g., hunger, disease, and war) and preventative checks, which lower the birth rate (e.g., abortion, birth control, prostitution, celibacy, and the postponement of marriage).[4]

It was heady, controversial stuff. It captured the public imagination. Even ordinary people started to wonder whether he didn't have a point. For many, optimism turned to doom and gloom.

Now suspend your disbelief for a moment. Let your imagination take flight. Picture yourself going back in time to 1798 and having a conversation with someone from that era—nobody special, just an ordinary citizen with a reasonable knowledge of the state of the world. Imagine how intelligent, wise, and all-knowing you would appear to that person.

You would be…a God!

Conversation One

England. Our glorious England, laid low by the spectre of hunger, famine, and disease. Is this the future that awaits our green and pleasant land?

No, it isn't.

What?! Who in heaven's name are you?

I am from a time and place that your mind cannot comprehend. I am your future. I am from the year 2013.

You jest, surely.

I do not jest, sir.

Why are you here?

To soothe your troubled mind. To allay the fears that you and so many of your countrymen harbour about the future of humanity.

How did you find me?

You found me. You summoned me across centuries of time so that I might be your salvation, so to speak. So that I might make you believe again.

7

Are you God?

You must be joking!

Who are you, then?

I am a mere mortal—an ordinary man from another time. My name is Bob.

I thought it was Ralph.

Why on earth would you say that?

It says so right there on your shirt—Ralph Lauren.

That's not my name.

You wear funny clothes, then.

You've got a once-in-a-lifetime chance to access the wisdom of the ages, and you're focusing on my clothes?!

You're a mere mortal. How can you impart wisdom and understanding to me?

The same way a father imparts wisdom and understanding to a child—by virtue of life experience.

You don't look as if you have much life experience. You certainly don't sound very wise.

> Perhaps. But right here, right now, I am possessed of the wisdom of eternity. Even a fraction of what I know would cause your head to explode—your cerebral hemispheres could not handle it.

I remain sceptical. Prove that you're from the future. Show me something from your time.

> Alright, then. I brought this along with me.

What is it?

> Ah, you're intrigued!

What a strange object. May I hold it?

> I'll let you have it at the end of our conversation. Do we have a deal?

A deal?

> An agreement.

Very well, then.

So tell me—what troubles you?

Thomas Malthus.

Ah! The famous Mr. Malthus.

You've heard of him?

Oh, yes! In my time, we still use the adjective that arose out of his name—Malthusian. You refer, naturally, to his famous work, *An Essay on the Principle of Population*, published this year.

Yes. He is, quite literally, the talk of the town. His predictions of famine and destruction have so permeated the intellectual fabric of society that we talk of little else. It is the subject of choice in newspapers, coffee shops, meeting halls, and the corridors of power. Never before has such a pall of gloom hung over England.

Malthus is wrong.

Now hang on a minute—that's a bit emphatic!

Perhaps. But it doesn't change the fact that he is wrong.

That's not what other people think.

It's still early days. His work has just been published. But over the next half-century, many great thinkers from around the world will challenge Mr. Malthus's views.

But Malthus is a brilliant man.

Brilliant men have been wrong before. Remember when brilliant men thought that the world was flat? Or that the sun revolved around the earth?

But his words resonate. He marshals a large body of evidence. He has constructed a well-formulated argument that is difficult to refute.

The rate of growth of population is greater than the rate of growth of food production. We're breeding faster than our ability to feed ourselves. Therefore we must run out of food one day, and famine will do the rest.

Exactly—you have summarised it well.

It's a tempting theory. But it's wrong.

Prove it.

Well, I'm here, aren't I?

That's not an argument!

Take it from me: humanity is alive and well in the twenty-first century, stuffing their faces on every conceivable occasion, shoehorning their way into clothes that no longer fit, and hitting the gym every day in a vain attempt to shed weight.

I have absolutely no idea what you have just said.

Sorry—I got a bit carried away there. In the future, there is more than enough food to go around. And it is cheap. In many countries, the problem isn't starvation—it's obesity.

How can this be? There must be at least two billion people on the planet in your time.

It's just over seven billion.

Seven billion souls? And there's enough food for all of them?!

There is so much food that we throw it away.

That must mean hundreds of millions of horses to plough the fields, which must surely take up every square mile of the country. Every man, woman, and child must be labouring all day and all night to produce the volumes of food you talk about.

Hah—that's your mistake right there!

My mistake?

Well, Mr. Malthus's mistake.

And what is the mistake, pray?

The assumption that nothing changes. That because every man and his horse are working the land in back-breaking toil today, it will continue to be so tomorrow.

It will not?

Over the next fifty years, everything will change. England will see new methods of agriculture that will make Thomas Malthus's predictions seem comically wrong.[5]

How?

In a word—productivity. You will be able to produce more food, using fewer people and less land.

But that defies all logic!

No, it doesn't. There is already precedent for it right here in England—your textile industry has massively increased its productivity through mechanisation. Think of machines like the Spinning Jenny and the Mule, which have allowed England to produce more textiles of better quality, using far fewer people.

Yes, but that's a manufacturing process. This is about food.

And how is food different?

In every way. Do you grow your own vegetables?

No. I buy them at the supermarket. That's a big store, by the way.

So I gathered. Well, I plant my own vegetables, I'll have you know. In my back garden.

Thank you for sharing that with me.

If I wanted to increase my output of vegetables, I would need more of everything, not less. I would have to work more, plant more, and use more of my garden. So your utopian logic escapes me.

Let's try a different tack. Do you have a well on your property?

Why do you ask?

Humour me. Do you have a well on your property?

No.

Okay, let's imagine that you'd like to dig a well. A very basic one. Say about ten feet deep. Just far enough for you to hit water.

Okay.

Now let's imagine that the only people available are you and me. And we don't have any tools. We can only use our bare hands and whatever rocks or stones we can find.

That wouldn't be easy.

No, it wouldn't. How long do you reckon it would take us?

One or two days? Perhaps longer?

Right. Now imagine someone hands us a spade. We'd be able to dig that hole in far less time, right? Perhaps only half a day?

Perhaps.

And what would happen if we were given a second spade?

We would both be able to dig and finish the job in an hour or two.

Or you could do it on your own, and I could go and do something else.

Such as what?

Dig a second well. Go shoot a pheasant for dinner. Or even go work and earn some money.

And your point?

Simply this—productivity frees people up to do other things.

So I've got my well, and we're eating pheasant for dinner...

Sarcasm is good. Stay with me—and you're going to have to take a leap of faith here. Imagine that the spade didn't require you to operate it. It is effectively a machine. It works without human intervention.

Oh, come on!

And what's more, this miracle machine digs at such a phenomenal rate that the well could be completed in a few minutes.

That's nonsense!

I know all of this is difficult for you to grasp, but our imaginary example of digging a well will one day be seen in agriculture—and sooner than you think.

You're surely making this up as you go along.

You need to keep an open mind here. A new range of farming tools and machines will be invented that will transform everything, from ploughing and planting to harvesting and threshing. These farming tools will first be drawn by horses and then by something called a tractor. Food will be produced on a scale hitherto unimaginable—

A tractor?!

Yes. It's essentially a horseless vehicle that moves under its own power. Well, to be specific, it's powered by something called an internal combustion engine, which draws its energy from oil, which is pumped up from underground, refined and…you're not getting this, are you?

No.

It's too far beyond your time. Here's the bottom line—

The bottom line?

Here's what you need to know: the mechanisation of agriculture means far fewer people will be required to feed the nation. It will free up hundreds of thousands of people to work in other areas of the economy, provide manpower for the army and navy, and make England prosperous and powerful.

Even if everything you say is true—and I must confess that I have trouble believing it—there's still one thing I don't understand.

What's that?

The "productivity" of the food itself. A potato is a potato. A cabbage is a cabbage. It's not suddenly going to get any bigger. Or more plentiful.

Says who?

Thomas Malthus. And I quote: We may be quite sure that among plants, as well as among animals, there is a limit to improvement.[6]

Be sceptical about people who profess to be sure of anything.

A given area of land can't suddenly start yielding more food.

Oh, yes, it can.

That makes no sense. It's as if a woman, instead of giving birth to one child at a time, were suddenly able to produce ten all at once with each pregnancy.

I like the parallel that you draw! That's exactly what will happen. The land will become more fertile. It will yield more fruit and vegetables with each planting.

How the devil will that happen?

Do you know how you cross-breed various dogs to produce a specific type of dog that has certain desirable characteristics? Say strength, agility, or the ability to hunt?

Yes—I myself have a cross-bred terrier.

Well, in the next fifty years, you will know how to do that with plants.

Really?

The pioneering work of people like Charles Darwin and Gregor Mendel—names that mean nothing to you now, but will to your children—will usher in a new, advanced science of plant breeding.[7] You'll be able to make plants that are strong, bountiful, and resistant to certain types of disease and weather.

Amazing!

That's just the tip of the iceberg. New crop rotation systems will mean that you won't need to have so much land lying fallow between planting seasons. New crops will give more yield per acre. Better irrigation systems will allow for longer growing seasons. New kinds of fertilizer will produce vast new tracts of arable land—you'll even be able to plant on wasteland. New improved livestock that can be fed throughout the winter will give larger yields of meat.

Ye Gods!

By the time we get to my era in the twenty-first century, the proportion of the population in England involved in agriculture will be a mere 1 to 2 percent. That compares with around 60 percent today.[8]

I don't know what to say. I don't know what to believe.

Believe in your future. What's the world population now, in your time— about one billion people?

Maybe slightly less.

No matter—let's deal in round numbers. How many times do you think it will double between now and the twenty-first century?

Well, you said earlier that the world population in your time is just over seven billion. So it will have doubled from one billion to two billion, then from two billion to four billion, and finally from four billion to just over seven billion.

Well, during all that time, food production will not just keep pace with population growth, but will actually exceed it.

Does nobody starve in your time?

Yes, they do, but it's because of political instability and lack of economic opportunity, not any inherent inability to produce food.

Are you saying people are allowed to starve by their leaders?

Basically, yes. We have a saying in our time: there are no famines in countries that have a free press.

I'll take comfort in that statement later today when I read my copy of The Times.

Here's a final statistic: in 1798, as you and I speak, an agricultural worker produces enough food to feed just you and me. In the twenty-first century, an agricultural worker produces enough food to feed you, me, and at least twenty-five other people living down the road![9]

You have an amazing ability to conjure up facts and figures as if out of thin air.

I get it off Google.

Google?

You've heard of the oracle at Delphi, in ancient Greece?

Yes. It was a shrine built around an ancient spring. Delphi was considered the centre of the world. People came from all over Greece and beyond to have their questions answered there by the priestess of Apollo.

Well, Google is similar. In my time, everyone has access to it, wherever they may be. You ask it a question, and it gives you an answer.

Is it also in Greek?

No, but sometimes it's all Greek to me...

Does it predict the future?

No one can predict the future. The future is unknowable. That's why it's called the future. Otherwise it would be called the present. So it's foolish to worry about it.

Mr. Malthus is a fool, then?

No, Mr. Malthus is a very clever man. But he is only human. And all humans are bound by the limits of knowledge of their time. Or, to put it another way, we don't know what we don't know.

Aren't you forgetting something?

What?

That!

Oh, yes—the object from my time.

What is it?

Try and figure it out. Here—hold it in your hands.

What a strange material. Smooth, durable, yet not heavy at all.

Everything weighs a lot less in the future.

What does it do? I can see no earthly use for it.

It produces light.

To produce light, you need a candle or an oil lamp—in short, a source of flame. Where is the flame?

There is no flame.

Then there can be no light.

See that button over there? Press it.

Nothing's happening.

No, you've got to slide it too. Like this—see?

Oh, heavens above! Bright, clean light! And of a purity that is not of this world! Look—the beam travels wherever you point it! It lights up the deepest recesses of my room!

We call it a torch.

But how is the light produced? Where does the fuel come from?

It's all inside. Trust me.

What happens if I switch it off? Will the light come back?

Try it and see.

It does come back! This is nothing short of miraculous! Even my wife could operate this.

Don't shine it in my face—you're blinding me!

Sorry. So do homes in your time have hundreds of these torches?

Oh, no. Our homes aren't lit by torches. Very few people even own torches. They're more of an emergency tool.

How could you choose not to use such a clever invention? What could possibly be better than this?

Overhead electric light. But we're getting ahead of ourselves.

Won't you tell me more?

I can't. I have to leave.

I was just getting used to you.

Sorry.

Can I keep the torch?

I'm afraid not. But you'll be able to tell people about it.

They would take me for a lunatic.

They probably would. Look, I can feel myself being pulled away...

Where are you going?

Another conversation is calling.

Where? With whom?

I could tell you, but you wouldn't believe me...

CHAPTER 2
The Coal Scare

In the increasing depth and difficulty of coal mining, we shall meet that vague but inevitable boundary that will stop our progress.

WILLIAM STANLEY JEVONS

England

~

1865

Today, in the twenty-first century, many people have never seen a lump of coal in their lives. With our petrol-powered cars, electrically driven trains and centrally heated homes, we are unlikely to come into contact with it unless we live near a coal mine or work in a coal-fired power station. In the public eye, coal plays second fiddle to oil as the world's major source of energy.

But in the mid-1800s, at the height of the Industrial Revolution, coal was the world's primary source of energy. It fuelled the steam engines and machinery that powered the momentous changes occurring in agriculture, manufacturing, mining and transportation. It was a period of world economic growth—led by England, the dominant power of the day—that led to unparalleled improvements in industrial productivity, workers' wages, and the lot of ordinary people.

But could the bonanza continue? One man seemed to think that it wouldn't. He was William Stanley Jevons, a British economist and logician. He published *General Mathematical Theory of Political Economy* in 1862, and *A Serious Fall in the Value of Gold* in 1863.[1]

But it was in 1865 that he became well known with the publication of *The Coal Question,* which first planted in the public mind the possibility that the coal might not last forever. He asked whether it was wise to allow commerce to go on flourishing beyond the point at which it could reasonably be sustained.

The full title of his book was: *The Coal Question: An Enquiry Concerning the Progress of the Nation, and the Probable Exhaustion of our Coal Mines.* It starts with a powerful description of the wonders of coal, and of society's insatiable appetite for it:

> Coal in truth stands not beside but entirely above other commodities. It is the material energy of the country—the universal aid—the factor in everything we do. With coal, almost any feat is possible or easy; without it, we are thrown back into the laborious poverty of early times.[2]

But coal reserves were not unlimited, Jevons argued. Over time, it gets harder to mine, even as demand continues to grow exponentially.

> I must point out the painful fact that such a rate of growth will before long render our consumption of coal comparable with the total supply. In the increasing depth and difficulty of coal mining, we shall meet that vague but inevitable boundary that will stop our progress.[3]

Jevons estimated that available resources were not sufficient for even one hundred years, and that long before that, the prosperity and wealth of society would begin to decline.

> Suppose our progress to be checked within half a century, yet by that time our consumption will probably be three or four times what it now is; there is nothing impossible or improbable in this; it is a moderate supposition, considering that our consumption has increased eightfold in the last sixty years. But how shortened and darkened will the prospects of the country appear, with mines already deep, fuel dear, and yet a high rate of consumption to keep up if we are not to retrograde.[4]

And echoing the Malthusian thinking that still pre-vailed at the time, Jevons pointed out that population growth would continue to increase even as the coal started to run out.

> Prosperity, in terms of per capita consumption, would therefore fall.[5]

The outlook was bleak. Society should start preparing for the worst and use the time available to make some important changes.

> We may spend [our current material wealth] on the one hand in increased luxury and ostentation and corruption, and we shall be blamed. We may spend it on the other hand in raising the social and moral condition of the people, and in reducing the burdens of future generations. Even if our succes-sors be less happily placed than ourselves, they will not then blame us.[6]

The far-reaching implications of *The Coal Question* weighed on the minds of the intellectuals of the day. One of them is deep in conversation with Bob...

Conversation Two

So tell me—what troubles you?

The end.

The end?

We are the most powerful nation in the world. Our wealth is unsurpassed. Our ships rule the waves. Our factories supply the world—there is virtually no product, however small, that does not carry the mark Made in England. The ingenuity of our inventors knows no bounds: we are responsible for the steam engine, the telegraph service, and the first transatlantic cable. Beneath my feet run the trains of the London Underground Railway, the first of its kind in the world. Ours is truly a greatness of historic proportions. And it all depends on the continued availability of cheap coal. You ask what troubles me? The possibility that it could all end when the coal runs out. That's what troubles me.

If the coal runs out.

Pardon?

If the coal runs out—do not assume that it will.

But it surely must.

Why—just because William Stanley Jevons says so?

He is a smart man. He knows a lot.

I know more.

You are very arrogant.

I apologise—I do not mean to be.

Here is an eminent economist, one of the intellectual giants of our time, advancing a compelling argument that has caught the imagination of the nation. Why do you dismiss it in so cavalier a fashion?

Because it is flawed. Because it is simplistic. Because it ignores the lessons of history.

The lessons of history?

To make sense of the future, you have to understand the past. To make sense of where coal is going, you must first understand its beginnings. Do you?

Do you mean when man first started using coal?

Not just when, but why. In economics, it's all about motive. Always look for the why.

Okay, why did we first start using coal on a major scale?

Because it was better than the alternative.

And what was the alternative?

Wood.

I'm not quite with you.

People don't start using a particular energy source just for the hell of it. There is always a good reason. Let's imagine you're on a desert island. You need to build a fire for warmth. What would you use?

Well, wood. It would be easy to cut, collect, and store.

Good. And if there was coal on the island? Would you consider it? After all, coal burns better and longer than wood.

I might—if it was easily accessible, and I didn't have to dig for it.

And if it wasn't?

Well, then I'd stay with the wood.

A rational choice. Now imagine you're on the island for so long that you start to use up all the wood. What would you do now?

I'd switch to coal.

Again, a rational choice.

You use that word a lot—rational.

That's because ultimately, all economic choices are rational choices. That's exactly how coal usage started in England. Where it was easily accessible, people used it. The Romans used coal on their northern England frontier along Hadrian's Wall in the coal-bearing districts of Northumberland to heat homes, barracks, villas, and baths. In other areas at other times, peasants dug small surface pits locally for domestic fuel. But it was the exception.[7]

Are you saying that most of the time, people preferred wood?

Yes. It was abundant. And it was far more accessible than coal. For hundreds of years, entire forests were felled to provide wood to build homes, castles, cathedrals, ships, mills, machinery, and barrels for storing food and drink. It was used as fuel for lime-burning, glass-making, brewing, and domestic fires. Wood was everywhere. It was the energy source that underpinned civilization, much as coal is today.[8]

Then what happened?

The same thing that happens on your desert island—the wood started to run out. Prices skyrocketed. The world faced a timber crisis!

When, exactly?

The first records of severe shortages appear from around the thirteenth century. In parts of France, the price of wooden coffins rose so high that poor families would hire them for the burial service, and the undertaker would dig up the corpse afterwards and recycle the coffin. Writers in England and France were starting to highlight what they described as the "assault on the forests." Did you know that some four thousand oak trees were felled to build Windsor Castle in the fourteenth century?[9]

What a travesty!

It gets worse. In 1558, the city council of Stettin, a port on the Baltic, stopped its shipyards from building any more ships for outsiders because the supply of oak for Stettin's own merchant fleet was running short. After the great fire of London in 1666, there wasn't enough timber locally to rebuild the city—virtually all of the wood had to be imported. Large stretches of forests in England were set aside as strategic assets.[10]

That certainly qualifies as a crisis.

I'll say! The great nations of Europe were now faced with a stark choice. They could either import timber from Scandinavia and Eastern Europe, or they could start switching to coal whenever possible.

And they chose the latter?

They did—it was a rational choice. The timber crisis was most acute in England from about 1570 to 1630. That's when we start to see an unwilling but dramatic change to coal as the nation's industrial fuel. Demand for coal was highest in London and the densely populated area around it, because that's where wood was in shortest supply.[11]

And what was done after that?

Well, nothing.

What do you mean, "nothing"?

Exactly that—nothing. Nobody had to do anything. Supply and demand took over.

Ah, the eternal law of economics!

Actually, it's a law of human behaviour, but let's not nit-pick. Anyway, more and more coal was produced, so its price came down. Coal started to be cheaper than wood. So people stopped using wood.

You make it sound simple.

It is simple. In real terms, the price of coal to consumers in London fell by 40 percent over the course of the Industrial Revolution, from around 1700 to 1860, yet coalfield annual output expanded eighteenfold.[12]

That's quite astounding.

And it wasn't just price. Efficiency came into it too.

What do you mean?

Consider this: Today, in the 1860s, England burns mainly coal for its energy, right?

Right.

Now to obtain that same amount of energy by burning firewood, you'd have to cut down a lot of trees, right?

Right.

How much land do you reckon would have to go under cultivation to plant those trees?

Surprise me.

About twenty-five million acres.[13]

Good heavens — that's nearly the entire farmland of England!

Yep. To coin a phrase from my time, coal gives you more bang for your buck.

So the decision to use coal rather than wood was pretty much clear-cut, it seems.

It was a no-brainer.

The sense of your colourful metaphors eludes me, but no matter. So if I understand you correctly, you're going to tell me that Jevons is correct, and that we'll start to run short of coal just like we ran short of timber. Right?

Wrong.

You are exasperating!

You are jumping to conclusions.

Why did you spend all this time explaining the timber crisis, then?

Simply to show you that a shortage of anything isn't a big deal—over time, people will always find a solution. All that matters is that they be free to explore alternatives, and that prices are free to reflect abundance or scarcity.

That still leaves us with Jevons and his analysis. Will the coal run out, yes or no?

You're asking the wrong question.

What do you mean?

> You're framing your question in terms of a negative scenario. We've just seen with the timber crisis that society will always adapt to whatever energy source it needs at any given time. So you need to reframe and ask a positive question.

I'm still not following you.

> Instead of asking whether the coal will run out—because it might not necessarily run out—why not ask if there is perhaps a reason why we might not want to use coal any more.

Well, is there a reason?

> Yes.

I can't see it.

> Let's go back to our desert island. If you recall, we were at the stage where you were using wood to make fire. Right?

Right.

Then you switched to coal when the wood started to run out. Right?

Right.

So you're on your desert island, burning coal, and keeping warm and happy. There's more than enough of it. Then one day, you decide you don't need coal anymore. Why? What could possibly prompt you to make such a momentous decision?

I'll be damned if I know.

This is like pulling teeth. Think, man!

I give up.

You stop using coal because you discover a new energy source.

A new energy source?!

Yes.

What new energy source?

We'll get to that in a minute. Let's recap. You're on your desert island. You've stumbled upon a new, better energy source that's easily accessible. Do you accept, therefore, that you might stop using coal?

I might. Yes.

Well, that's exactly what's going to happen in the not-too-distant future here in England and Europe. You will see it in your lifetime. This new form of energy will completely transform your economy.

What is this new form of energy? Coal powers our ships, drives our steam engines, and heats our homes. What could possibly be better than coal?

Oil and electricity.

Oil and electricity? But these are not new sources of energy! Both here and in North America, we have been burning refined oil for more than twenty years as a cheap alternative to whale oil; and drilling for oil is now quite common around the world.[14] As for electricity, there has been much pioneering work in the field this century from scientists such as Michael Faraday and James Clerk Maxwell.[15]

You are correct. Strictly speaking, these aren't new sources of energy. However, they are in their infancy. In the next twenty to thirty years, they will be catapulted to a new level of maturity on the back of two inventions that will change the world.

And what are these inventions? I would have thought mankind had already reached the pinnacle of ingenuity!

And you call me arrogant! The first invention is the internal combustion engine.

That's a bit of a mouthful.

Let me try to explain it to you in present-day terms that you will understand. You are familiar with the steam engine, are you not?

I am. Water is heated in a confined space until it turns to steam, and the steam is used to drive a piston which produces mechanical power.

An eloquent, succinct explanation! In an internal combustion engine, a mixture of petroleum and air is compressed in a confined space, and then an electrical spark is applied to it. The force produced by the explosion is used to drive a piston, which produces mechanical power.

I fail to see much of a difference.

Ah, but there is, you see! This new type of engine is much, much lighter and is far more efficient.

How so?

Well, to produce steam, a steam engine needs the water to be constantly boiling. So there has to be a fire going all the time, fed by coal. That's how your locomotives work—you've got a couple of men constantly shovelling coal into the burner. Then there's the sheer size of the thing—it's made of solid steel and weighs a ton.

And this is not the case with the internal combustion engine?

No, it's a whole new ballgame.

Ballgame?!

It's a totally novel concept. There's no need for a fire to be going all the time. So it's much lighter. And the energy produced by the explosion of the fuel-air mixture is significant. So the engine doesn't have to be very big—barely the size of a suitcase.

It certainly sounds like a significant development. Perhaps I would be more excited if I could envision how this would change the face of society, as you so confidently say it will.

I feel I'm losing you here, so I'm going to keep this short. In 1885, a German by the name of Karl Benz will invent a wheeled vehicle that carries its own internal combustion engine. I'm going to repeat that last bit so that you can grasp the significance of it—that carries its own internal combustion engine.

Which means it can go anywhere?

Not just anywhere, but under its own power.

A horseless carriage!

Exactly—a horseless carriage! Its formal name is automobile, but it will come to be known as the motor car.

And this new kind of engine will replace all the engines that are currently powered by coal?

Pretty much. After the wheel, the internal combustion engine is arguably the most significant technological development in the history of the world. It will power all manner of machines and modes of transport that you could not even imagine at this stage. It will utterly transform the way people live.

Speak to me about the other big development — electricity.

In 1884, about the same time as the invention of the motor car, one of your eminent engineers, Sir Charles Parsons, will invent something called a steam turbine. Suffice to say it is a superior form of steam engine with fewer moving parts. These turbines will be used to drive electro-mechanical generators that will produce vast amounts of electricity that will heat your homes, light your streets, power your factories, and drive your ships.

So the great coal problem that Jevons writes about actually becomes a non-issue?

A very big non-issue. It becomes OBE'd.

OBE'd?

Overtaken By Events. It's a term I like using.

So does this great wave of innovation spell the end of the coal industry?

> Not at all. Coal has a bright future ahead of it. We will uncover more and more of it, and have the ability to mine it far more easily than today. In the twenty-first century, coal still accounts for a big slice of the world's energy consumption.

So Jevons is doubly wrong, then. He's wrong to think that the coal might run out, and he's wrong to think that it's the only answer to our industrial might.

> Well, that's what happens when you engage in static-state thinking.

Is that another of your favourite terms?

> It is. Static-state thinking is a peculiar condition that afflicts all catastrophe theorists, from Malthus to Jevons. It is the assumption that society remains static, that nothing changes, and that we are incapable of adapting to new circumstances.

Indeed, it is peculiar. After all, the history of mankind is the history of movement. Everything moves: the planets, the tides, and the seasons—even our very growth as human beings from cradle to grave.

I see we are finally on the same page. It is most heartening. I feel that Jevons, bright man as he is, should have had a look at his garden before writing his book.

His garden? I fail to comprehend the parallel that you draw.

Well, look at a garden. On the surface, nothing's happening. But underneath the soil, it's a different story. Seeds are germinating, roots are spreading, and new growth is ready to break through. Society is like that.

I get your drift. Growth, change, and innovation—it all happens out of sight?

Yes, but it eventually breaks through. And when it does, it is always a beautiful picture.

I'm ready now.

Ah, yes. The object from my time. It always gets people's attention.

What have you brought?

Something unexpected. Here—don't drop it.

But it's just…a box!

> Ah, but not any old box. Run your fingers along the surface.

What a strange material! Shiny, smooth and not heavy at all.

> Everyone says that!

Who's everyone?

> Never mind. So what do you think it is?

I have not the foggiest notion. It seems to serve no useful purpose that I can discern.

> There's that reaction again. You're all so practical—always looking for a useful purpose.

Well, why else would anyone go to the trouble of producing this?

> For fun? For enjoyment? For learning?

Are you going to tell me what to do with this?

Do you like music?

I love music.

Well, this will play music for you.

Do you take me for a fool? Where are the musical instruments? Where is the orchestra?

Inside. Press that button there.

The one marked "CD?"

Yes.

What's a CD?

Don't ask.

Okay. I've pressed the button. Now what?

Turn that knob marked "Volume" down a bit—we don't want to shatter your eardrums.

Fine. I still don't hear the music.

Now press "Play." I hope you like Mozart.

The Coal Scare

Oh, my God!

Isn't that amazing?

What rapturous music!

Makes you forget about coal, doesn't it?

Where is the energy source? I don't detect any heat.

No—don't turn it over!

But it has to have an energy source!

It does. And it's not coal.

What is it, then? What powers this unearthly contraption?

Electricity. It's battery-powered.

Battery-powered?!

It's a long story. Just enjoy the music while you can.

Why—are you about to leave?

Very shortly, alas. I have people to see. Minds to change.

Where will you go?

Wherever I am called. And to pre-empt your next question—no, you can't keep the music box.

But people will not believe me when I tell them about it.

I wouldn't even try to convince them. You'd just be certified as a lunatic.

We started off discussing coal, and we ended up with music. What's the connection?

None. I just wanted to show you how unpredictable and exciting the future is.

Will I see the CD player in my time?

No, but you will have the gramophone soon, in 1877. And that's a good start.

CHAPTER 3
The Horse-Manure Scare

The presence of so many horses constantly moving through the streets is a very serious matter.

Popular Science Monthly

New York

~

1900

Next time you watch a Hollywood movie that is set in nineteenth-century London or New York, when horse-drawn transport was still the norm, take a closer look—you'll notice that the streets are clean, the air is pure and wholesome, and people go about their business in a pristine environment.

This is a romanticised picture. You might think that back then, the general level of urban hygiene was high. It most certainly wasn't.

At the end of the nineteenth century and the beginning of the twentieth century, writers in the popular and scientific media were hammering away at the problem of urban pollution caused by horses and demanding that they be banned from American cities. This was no trivial demand, given that there were about 3.5 million horses in cities across the country.

They represented an environmental health problem of staggering proportions, because of the huge quantities of horse manure and urine that had to be cleaned up each day.[1]

Over in London, England, children known as "crossing sweepers" would help well-attired ladies and gentlemen to cross the street by sweeping up the muck in front of them. No such service was offered in more egalitarian America.

In 1885, an engineer, Francis V. Greene, made a study of urban traffic conditions in New York City at the intersection of Broadway and Pine Street. On a typical day, he counted 7,811 horse-drawn vehicles passing the busy corner, many with teams of two or more horses.[2] One can easily imagine the stench. It was noisy too. In the 1890s, a writer in *Scientific American* noted that the sounds of traffic on busy New York streets made conversation nearly impossible.

Writing in *Popular Science Monthly* in 1892, the United States Commissioner of Labor, Caroll D. Wright, left no doubt as to where she stood on the issue:

> The presence of so many horses constantly moving through the streets is a very serious matter. The

vitiation of the air by the presence of so many animals is alone a sufficient reason for their removal,
while the clogged condition of the streets impedes
business, and involves the safety of life and limb.[3]

In 1908, one writer described the one hundred thou-
sand-plus horses in New York City as

an economic burden, an affront to cleanliness, and
a terrible tax upon human life.[4]

But salvation was on the way in the form of the motor
car. The media threw its weight behind this marvel-
lous new invention. Journals such as *Harper's Weekly*,
Lippincott's Magazine, and *Scientific American* were
filled with articles extolling the virtues of the car.[5]
Munsey's Magazine wrote:

The horse has become unprofitable. He is too
costly to buy and too costly to keep.[6]

A writer in *American City* echoed this theme:

It is all a question of dollars and cents, this gaso-
line or oats proposition. The automobile is no longer classed as a luxury. It is acknowledged to be
one of the great time-savers in the world.[7]

The automobile eventually started to invade American cities. Streets became cleaner and quieter. The number of flies was greatly reduced. Everything moved at a faster pace. It was no contest—the car beat the horse hands-down.

But in 1900, the miracle was still at least a decade away. People still had to deal with horse manure. This reality weighs on the mind of the next person Bob talks to, a New York bank manager who's clearly had enough of the equine presence on New York streets.

Conversation Three

So tell me—what troubles you?

A public health crisis that could spell the end of urban living as we know it.

I am vaguely familiar with the problem. Enlighten me.

Horse manure plagues all large cities in the world. An oft-quoted article in The Times of London of 1894 ventured that if nothing is done, every street in the city will be buried in nine feet of horse manure by 1950.[8]

Oh, I wouldn't lend much credence to these long-range predictions. None other than Alexander Graham Bell himself is said to have predicted that one day, every town in America will have a telephone.[9]

He is wrong?

Yes, but not in the way you think. We digress. Tell me more about this public health crisis.

Our streets are strewn with horse manure and run yellow with rivers of horse urine. Our cities are noisy with the incessant clattering of iron shoes on cobblestone streets. The air hums with the constant buzzing of flies and assaults the nostrils with a pervasive stench that never lets up.

It is not a pretty picture.

It is a Faustian bargain, a deal with the devil! It is the price mankind must pay for the progress of the past hundred years.

That's a harsh assessment!

Is it? The only reason we have all these horses is because we have all these people. And the people have all flocked to the cities because of opportunity. And the opportunity has been created by the Industrial Revolution, the continued rise of free-market capitalism, and the ever-increasing wealth of the general population.

That's a good thing, surely?

Well, yes and no. From 1800 to 1900, the United States per capita Gross Domestic Product has shot up nearly five times. Our urban population has swelled by some thirty million people. All of this means more trade. But trade means goods, and all goods, at some point, have to be transported by horse.[10]

What about the railroads?

They are not the panacea we all thought they'd be.

Why not?

Well, think about it: nearly every item shipped by rail needs to be collected and distributed by horses at both ends of the journey. So as rail shipments have boomed, so has urban traffic. Guess who tends to own the largest fleets of horses in the big cities?[11]

The railway companies?

Exactly.

So what is the solution that your experts are proposing?

There is no solution. At least none that we can see. Our best urban planners have put their heads together and come up empty-handed. We can't exactly disinvent horse-drawn transport, can we? Do you know how many horses we have here in New York? More than one hundred thousand!

That's a frightening statistic.

Not as frightening as the filth that goes with it. How much manure do you think a horse drops every day?

I have no idea.

Go on — take a guess.

Ten pounds?

Try fifteen to thirty pounds.

Thirty pounds? That's nearly the weight of a three-year-old child!

On any given day, the city has to clean up two to three million tons of horse manure, not to mention about twenty thousand gallons of urine. And do you know what happens to the manure in extreme weather?

I'm not so sure I want to know…

In wet weather, the streets are turned into swamps of muck that you would not want to put your foot into no matter how good your shoes. In dry weather, it turns to dust, which is then whipped up by the wind, choking pedestrians, and coating buildings. And summer's the worst, because the farmers are unable to leave their crops to come and collect all the dung.[12] *So guess what?*

It piles up?

And how! Vacant lots in cities across the country are dotted with piles of dry horse manure that rise up to fifty feet into the air.[13] *A monument to our folly—both literally and figuratively.*

I can easily imagine the stench.

You're not imagining it—it's real. Can you hear that buzzing sound outside?

Flies?

Swarms of them. About three billion flies hatch in horse manure every day in cities across the United States. In fact, outbreaks of deadly infectious diseases like typhoid and infant diarrhea are always traced to spikes in the fly population.[14] *Are you feeling despondent yet?*

I'm getting there.

Then let me help you along, because the litany of problems that arise from the presence of horses is never-ending. They cause accidents by kicking, biting, or trampling bystanders. They often fall on slippery roads and are too heavy to be lifted up and taken away—so they're shot and the corpses are left to rot, because then they become easier to saw into pieces and cart off. And the cruelty is heart-rending: you'd think owners would take care of their horses because of the huge capital investment they represent. But they don't. It actually makes financial sense for owners to rapidly work their horses to death.[15]

But why?

Because it costs such a lot to feed and care for them. An urban horse consumes tons of oats and hay, and needs around five acres of expensive urban land.[16]

Manure, urine, flies, noise, cruelty—I must confess that even I am taken aback by the sheer scale of the crisis.

After thousands of years of history, is this how it all ends—humanity drowning in the filth of its own progress? What do we do? You're supposed to be the wise one here. Tell me, what do we do?

Nothing.

Nothing? This crisis threatens the very foundations of society, and you say do nothing?!

Well, let me qualify that. Do what you can to get through the day. Feed and care for your horses. Clean the streets. Carry on with your business. But don't worry about the rest.

Don't worry?!

Trust that things are working out. The answer is unfolding right before your very eyes, but you fail to see it.

How so?

You're focused on the problem. So all you see is things getting worse. You need to be focused on things getting better.

I don't see how.

Flip the thing around. Assume there is an answer. Instead of asking how to stop the horse-manure problem from getting worse, ask what developments are happening around you that could make the horse-manure problem irrelevant.

Irrelevant?

In the sense that it won't matter anymore.

You mean it becomes a non-issue?

Yes. The output of horse manure will decrease naturally, without anyone having to decree it. Your streets will become clean again.

I see.

Well go on, then. Ask the question.

What developments are happening around us that could make the horse-manure problem irrelevant?

Well, it's already out there in the streets. Look past the horse manure.

Electrically driven streetcars?

Exactly! Right here in Brooklyn, you have been running an electrified streetcar line since 1890.[17] It may not seem like a big development, but it's a significant start. Electrification of mass transport is slowly gathering pace here in New York.

It's not about to replace the horse anytime soon.

Don't be so sure.

And what makes you so sure?

I know what's coming. You don't.

Like what, for example?

Okay. There's something big happening in the field of public transport right now, in 1900. Even a sceptic like you must surely be aware of it.

The construction of the New York subway?

Yes! It's the city's first electrically powered underground railway system. When it starts operating in 1904, it's going to carry a hundred thousand passengers on its very first day! They'll be whisked along at speeds of forty miles per hour. That compares to a mere six miles per hour by trolley in the streets.[18]

That's incredible!

And it'll usher in the electrification of your elevated trains too. Within the next five years, electricity will be playing a role in public transport that nobody would have imagined.

Is this the end of the horse-manure crisis?

No, but it is the beginning of the end. The real revolution that's going to take the horse off the streets, both in cities and the countryside, is something different altogether.

What?

Again, look around you. What form of transportation do you see that wasn't there about ten years ago?

You're not referring to the motor car?

I am.

Oh, come on! It's a toy—a plaything for rich people.

Do you know how many cars were sold in America this year?

A couple of hundred?

Just over four thousand.[19]

Still a paltry number. And all owned by the wealthy. Ordinary folk would never be able to afford one.

Never say never when it comes to new technology. They will be able to afford a car soon, thanks to a very clever and enterprising man called Henry Ford.

And what's his claim to fame?

The Model T. In exactly eight years' time, in 1908, he will launch the first car to be mass-produced on moving assembly lines using interchangeable parts, and it will be marketed to the middle class.[20]

You lost me at assembly lines.

Don't worry. All you need to understand is that he will build it faster, better, and cheaper than anyone else. He is living proof of the saying that if you build a better mousetrap, the world will beat a pathway to your door.

Cars replacing horses? It doesn't feel real.

Oh, it's real, alright. Barely two years after its launch, the Model T will be rolling off the production line at three-minute intervals. By 1927, Mr. Ford will proudly watch the fifteen-millionth Model T come off the assembly line.[21] And do you know what will make all of this possible?

A desire to see the end of horse manure?

Horse manure will not even figure in people's buying decisions. It will all be about cost and convenience. The motor car will be cheaper to own and operate. And it will also be a whole lot more convenient and practical—the rugged Model T will be able to travel along a muddy farm lane, ford a shallow stream, and even climb a steep hill.[22] If you'll pardon the pun, Mr. Ford will succeed in putting the car before the horse.

What an achievement!

It's his life's dream. Here's how he will describe it:

I will build a car for the great multitude. It will be large enough for the family, but small enough for the individual to run and care for. It will be constructed of the best materials, by the best men to be hired, after the simplest designs that modern engineering can devise. But it will be so low in price that no man making a good salary will be unable to own one—and enjoy with his family the blessing of hours of pleasure in God's great open spaces.[23]

I feel like owning one already!

Oh, you will soon. And so will many others. By 1932, the Ford Motor Company will be manufacturing one third of the world's automobiles.[24]

And the horse in all of this?

Gone from your city streets. Not all at once, but gradually. Freight haulage will be the last to go in the 1920s, with the advent of the motorised truck.[25] Ford will take society from horse power to horsepower—don't worry if you don't get that bit of wordplay. By the time you're in your old age, the most likely place you'll see a horse is on a farm, a ranch, or a racetrack.

The role of the horse as a beast of burden on city streets will finally be over?

Indeed. The car will be hailed as an environmental saviour. It will be seen as the technology that eradicated a major urban-planning nightmare that had brought society to the brink of despair.[26]

So the horse-manure crisis eventually turns out to be… well, a non-issue?

> Eventually, yes. Here and now, in your streets, there is a problem. But from a longer-term historical perspective, there is no problem—there is only change.

Don't get philosophical on me now.

> I have to. It's instructive. Do you like summer? I mean it can get fairly hot.

I love summer. As for the heat, that's the whole point of summer, isn't it?

> Exactly. Is summer a "problem" that you try to solve because it gets too hot?

Well, no.

> Of course not. You let summer run its course. What happens then?

Autumn sets in. The heat abates. The leaves fall from the trees.

> And again, you don't try and solve the "problem" of autumn. You don't run around shouting: "Oh, my

God, all the leaves are falling! We must stop the leaves from falling!"

Ha-ha. Very funny…

Autumn gives way to winter, winter gives way to spring, spring to summer, and the cycle starts again.

I sense you're about to make a point.

I am. From a broad historical perspective, progress moves in waves, or seasons. And it's only ever apparent with hindsight. A new way of doing things is discovered. It underpins society's advancement for a while. Then just when it looks as if it will be there forever, it is toppled from its perch as the next big innovation comes along.

And the cycle begins again.

Stone-age to iron-age.

Wood to coal.

Coal to oil and electricity.

Electricity to — ?

We don't know.

You don't?

Not yet. Even in my time, electricity is still the foundation of civilization. But it will change one day. It has to.

So when all's said and done, there is never anything to fear from the future?

Fear of the future is pointless. And it should certainly never be used as a basis for policy.

What is the hardest part of it all?

The transition. That uncomfortable period between the end of the old and the start of the new.

What advice would you give?

Know how to wait. Shakespeare put it best in Hamlet:

There is special providence in the fall of a sparrow. If it be now, 'tis not to come. If it be not to come, it will be now; if it be not now, yet it will come—the readiness is all.

Speaking of readiness—can I see the thing you promised to show me?

Patience, patience—here it is.

What a strange contraption! So light, so shiny, so smooth—and yet so strong.

I can't believe it—you're all reading from the same script!

What do you mean?

Never mind. Long story. What do you think this is?

It's got a glass window. It's got buttons going from one to nine. And it's called Nokia. I don't know—perhaps some sort of calculator?

Close. It can calculate, but that's not its primary function. Press any of the buttons.

Oh, that's interesting—the glass window has just come alive! It's a screen! And it shows a picture!

Any ideas?

Not a clue.

It's a phone.

A phone? I use a phone every day at the bank where I work. This is not a phone.

It is a phone. It's a mobile phone. You carry it with you.

It's far too small to be a phone. Where's the mouthpiece? Where's the rotary dial? Where are the wires?

It's all there. Just not in the way you're familiar with. Here, why don't you make a call?

How?

Dial the office.

Ah—that's interesting. The number is printed out as I type!

Now press the green button and hold it to your ear.

I can't hear anything.

Well, of course not, there's no signal.

No signal?

In the twenty-first century, the whole country is permeated by invisible phone signals that travel through the air, and through walls and buildings. If you have a phone, you can connect with other phones.

It would have been nice to see it work.

I know. But for now, try and appreciate the importance of it. What you're holding in your hands is going to revolutionise day-to-day communication in the future.

Will there be such a phone in every city?

That is such a funny question.

I am quite serious.

In my time, there are hundreds of millions of these phones around the country. Virtually every American has one.

They must all be very wealthy, then.

Why do you say that?

Because in New York today, only wealthy people can afford phones. I do not have one at home, yet I consider myself to be reasonably well off.

That will all change. In the future, phones will become so cheap that even maids and gardeners will be able to afford them. Some companies will even give them away.

Will cars have phones?

Yes, but—

What's that funny beeping noise? I thought you said there was no signal.

This is an alarm I set for myself.

But you are awake. Why would you need an alarm?

It's a reminder. It's telling me I have to go.

Go where?

Toward the end of the twentieth century, to a time you might yet see if you live to a ripe old age.

Here—don't forget your phone…

CHAPTER 4
The End-of-Civilisation Scare

*The battle to feed all of humanity is over. In the 1970s,
hundreds of millions of people will starve to death in spite
of any crash programs embarked on now.*

PAUL EHRLICH

New York

～

1975

I f the 1960s were the "swinging sixties," then the 1970s were perhaps the "sombre seventies." A perpetual mood of doom and gloom hung over much of the world.

The euphoria of the moon landings was long forgotten; fresher in the minds of most people was the oil crisis of 1973, when the big Arab oil producers launched an oil embargo against the United States and various European nations in retaliation for their support of Israel during the Yom Kippur war. For the first time in their history, Americans had to queue for petrol. Rationing was introduced. Fistfights, beatings, and stabbings broke out among frustrated motorists. Truck drivers went on strike, leaving food rotting in the fields and shortages in stores. A non-striking trucker was shot. Violence escalated. There were running battles with police in full riot gear.[1]

It was a time of big societal change too, with women's lib, black consciousness, gay pride, and legalised abortion all forcing their way onto the political agenda. It seemed like only yesterday that people still knew their place, listened to authority, and respected the social mores of the time. Crime, violence, and disorder soared in the big cities. New York was particularly bad, with City Hall on the edge of bankruptcy and the subway a filthy no-go area of tramps, muggers, and graffiti-adorned trains. The use of illicit drugs was rampant. Then in 1974, the Watergate political scandal erupted, forcing the resignation of President Richard Nixon. Confidence was eroded even further—if you couldn't trust the man in the White House, who could you trust?[2]

By 1975, the oil embargo was over, but the price at the pump kept on climbing. Inflation exploded. Unemployment rocketed. Confidence crumbled. It was no better in Britain, Canada, or Western Europe, where a long-term decline in manufacturing was setting in, leaving millions of blue-collar workers out of work. The 1970s were arguably the worst decade for the economies of the industrialised nations since the Great Depression of the 1930s. Terrorism surged around the world, with kidnappings, bombings, and hijackings. The very structure of society seemed to be crumbling before people's eyes, and no one could understand why.[3]

To make matters worse, the crisis was playing out against a background of environmental concern that the world was cooling and heading for a new ice-age, possibly by the end of the century.[4]

> The evidence in support of these predictions has now begun to accumulate so massively that meteorologists are hard-pressed to keep up with it,[5]

wrote *Newsweek*, in an article entitled "The Cooling World," in April 1975. It ended with a solemn warning:

> The longer the planners delay, the more difficult they will find it to cope with climatic change once the results become grim reality.[6]

Climate change, impending famine, exhaustion of the earth's natural resources—it was a heady cocktail of doom and gloom, and the media was happy to spread it around. Newspapers, radio, and television pumped out a steady stream of increasingly confident forecasts by some of the foremost political, scientific, and social commentators of the day. The theme was always the same—we have to curb population growth and rein in consumption to conserve resources. The bestselling books of the day carried titles like *The Late Great Planet Earth, Famine 1975!, The Population Bomb, The End of Affluence,* and *Limits to Growth.* They sold millions upon millions of copies to a troubled world desperate for answers.

Perhaps the most successful—and controversial—of this wave of authors was Paul Ehrlich, a professor from Stanford University. He captured the mood of the times with his bold, brash predictions on where the world was heading.[7] Eloquent, entertaining, and projecting an aura of intellectual infallibility, he preached his gospel in the media and became a household name.

The cover of his first book, *The Population Bomb*, set the scene with the following sentence just below the title:

> While you are reading these words, four people will have died from starvation. Most of them children.[8]

Inside, the book opened with the following unequivocal statement:

The battle to feed all of humanity is over. In the 1970s, hundreds of millions of people will starve to death in spite of any crash programs embarked upon now. At this late date, nothing can prevent a substantial increase in the world death rate.[9]

Both his books, *The Population Bomb* and *The End of Affluence* (which he co-wrote with his wife, Anne), influenced an entire generation. They also influence the next person Bob is in conversation with: a feisty, straight-talking New York university librarian who gives as good as she gets.

Conversation Four

So tell me—what troubles you?

Everything. Famine, disease, wars, the onward march of communism, inflation, gas shortages, the exhaustion of the earth's raw materials, global cooling—

Global cooling?!

It's all over the media. Time, Newsweek, The New York Times…

Look, lady: I'm going to play it straight with you. No kid gloves. Why do you believe all this stuff?

Well, why wouldn't I? People are starving in India. The Chinese are breeding like there's no tomorrow. The Russian threat grows stronger by the day. Inflation is higher than it's ever been. The price of gas is through the roof. And there's increasing consensus that we'll soon exhaust the earth's supplies of oil and mineral resources, and that we're heading for a new ice-age by the year 2000.

[Laughter.]

I'm glad you're finding this funny…

I'm sorry. I don't mean to be flippant.

These are life-and-death issues! This is the future of the planet that we're talking about!

I'm trying to keep a straight face here, really. But I just can't get over how you suspend all rational thought and allow yourself to be taken in by these ludicrous scenarios.

Okay, wise guy. Are you telling me that university professors, scientists, climatologists, researchers, government officials—not to mention the United Nations itself—are all wrong?

You know what? It's funny.

You're not answering my question. What's funny?

The fact that every single time some catastrophic vision of the future captures the imagination of the public, people always legitimise it by drawing attention to the intellectual pedigree of the people who advance it.

Huh?! Plain English, please...

It ain't true just because it's coming from an expert.

Well, if we can't trust the experts, who can we trust?

How about your own common sense? If a shabbily dressed tramp down on his luck knocks on your door and tells you the world will end in 1985, you'd laugh in his face, maybe give him a buck, and send him on his way. But when some expert with a university degree and a sharp suit barges into your living room on television and says the same thing, you lap it all up.

That's an unfair comparison!

Is it? Let me ask you something: do you know what you'll be doing five years from now, say, in March, 1980?

What do you mean?

Where you'll be working. Who you'll be living with. What car you'll be driving. In other words, do you know what your life will be like in March 1980?

Well, no. Obviously.

Why not?

Well, it depends on so many different things, doesn't it? My career, my health, when I finally get married, whether we decide to have kids, whether I take time out to do my PhD...

And if I asked the same question of anyone else, do you think they'd be able to tell me exactly what their personal lives will be like in five years' time?

Well, no.

Because, in your words, it depends on so many different things.

Yes.

So if you can't predict your own life five years from now, and nobody else can predict theirs either, how can anyone claim to be able to predict the life of the entire *planet*?!

Well, when you put it like that, it does seem a bit of a stretch.

What crystal ball are these guys gazing into? What makes them so special?

Mmm...

You're finally thinking. That's good. Be sceptical about people who claim to be able to predict the future. Do you read *The Economist?*

Do I look like an economist?!

Well, here's a tidbit from the future. In 1984, *The Economist* will ask sixteen people to make ten-year forecasts of economic growth rates, inflation rates, exchange rates, oil prices, and other key economic indicators. Four of the test subjects will be former finance ministers, four will be chairmen of multinational companies, four will be students from Oxford University, and four will be London dustmen.[10]

Dustmen?

Garbage collectors. A decade later, the magazine will review the forecasts and publish them. What do you think the findings will be?

You tell me.

Well, the finance ministers will be the worst. They'll come last in the accuracy of their predictions.

No kidding? Who will come first?

It will be a tie—between the garbage collectors and the company chairmen.[11]

No way!

You sound surprised. You shouldn't be. The future, by definition, is unknowable. So why would anyone accord any credibility to predictions about the future? They're not worth the paper they're written on.

Your assessment is rather harsh.

But you know it's right, don't you?

Intellectually, yes. Emotionally, no. Deep in my gut, I feel these experts are right. I mean their writing has struck a chord with millions of people. They're tapping into the mood of the times.

They're tapping into your fear.

Have you listened to the news lately? Can you blame us?

I guess not. I was at university in the 1970s. I remember the mood.

So you were also demonstrating against war, injustice, and the multinationals?

Actually, no. I was too busy trying to finish my assignments.

Did you not even read Marx?

Groucho, yes. Karl, no.

You're a real goody two-shoes, aren't you?

I'll take that as a compliment. Anyway, my point is that every one of the predictions of these doom-mongers is a worst-case scenario based on fear—fear of resources running out, fear of food running out, and fear of humanity not being able to change anything. Do you see a shrink?

Why do you ask?

You do, don't you!

Twice a week. How did you know?

Just a guess. Anyway, when you're at your shrink, lying on the couch—

Armchair.

Pardon?

Armchair. He doesn't have a couch.

Okay, when you're sitting in that armchair talking about your fears, your concerns, and your problems, what's his approach? Does he pander to your worst fears? Or does he try and give you hope?

Well, the latter. Obviously.

Exactly. No self-respecting psychologist would advise you to build your future on the assumption that your worst fears will be realised. You'd go into a spiral of depression. You'd be popping pills. You'd start drinking. Hell, you might even slit your wrists!

I can see where you're going with this.

Good, but I'm going to spell it out anyway. Fear is an extreme, negative emotion that clouds judgement in the worst possible way. All these doom merchants are in fear mode. They're not thinking straight. How old are you now?

Twenty-nine.

Well, by the time you're in your forties, it'll become apparent just how hopelessly off the mark they all are. Especially Ehrlich.

You don't seem to like Mr. Ehrlich very much.

It's not that at all. I'm sure he's a very nice man. I've seen him on television. Very entertaining.

But...I sense a "but" coming on.

But the sheer audacity of his predictions beggars belief. They're so outrageous as to be laughable.

Which ones are you referring to?

Where do I start? There are so many. How about this one from *The End of Affluence*—which, by the way, should have been called *The Beginning of Affluence*, for world growth, GDP, and general wealth all rose significantly in the following decades. Anyway, Ehrlich, ever modest, states:

One general prediction can be made with confidence: the cost of feeding yourself and your family will continue to increase. There may be minor fluctuations in food prices, but the overall trend will be up.[12]

And is the trend up?

> Of course it isn't. The price of food, as measured by the United Nations Food and Agriculture Organisation's extended real food-price index, will fall for twenty-five consecutive years between 1975 and 2000, even as the world's population increases from four billion to six billion people.[13]

Ooh, that is rather off the mark.

> Here's another gem:

> In our opinion, the last decades of the twentieth century will initiate a worldwide age of scarcity. There will be no more cheap abundant energy, no more cheap, abundant food, and soon the flow of cheap consumer goods will suffer increasing disruption and rising prices.[14]

Don't tell me—wrong on all three counts?

> Not just wrong—dead wrong. Food will get cheaper and more abundant. Oil will get cheaper and more abundant. Consumer goods will get cheaper and more abundant.

How much cheaper?

Between 1975 and 1999, the inflation-adjusted price of a barrel of oil will fall by more than 50 percent.[15] By the end of the century, US inflation will be three times lower than it is today.[16] Is that cheap enough for you?

Okay—no need to be smug.

Here's another. This is the one that'll make you laugh. Are you ready?

Shoot.

A run of miraculously good weather might delay it—perhaps for a decade, maybe even to the end of the century—but the train of events leading to the dissolution of India as a viable nation is already in motion.[17]

You're not laughing…

I don't get it.

Of course you don't! It's still 1975. You don't know this yet, but in the twenty-first century, India is one of the world's fastest-growing economies, a nuclear power, and one of the top food-producing nations. All savvy investors have India in their portfolio.

That's astounding!

Look, Ehrlich-bashing eventually gets tiresome. So let me end with this one.

If I were a gambler, I would take even money that England will not exist in the year 2000, and give 10 to one that the life of the average Briton would be of a distinctly lower quality than it is today.[18]

Go and find Paul Ehrlich and take him up on his bet!

England survives and thrives?

Everyone survives and thrives. The last decades of the twentieth century are a time of incredible growth, innovation, and change. In five years' time, China will embrace market reforms and unleash a wave of economic growth that will eventually lift hundreds of millions out of poverty and turn the country into an economic superpower. In the late 1980s, Russia will start to ditch communism, the Berlin Wall will fall, and the Eastern bloc countries will split off into independent states. A few years later, South Africa will phase out apartheid, release Nelson Mandela, and usher in a peaceful transition to democracy that will surprise the world.

The end of communism? The end of apartheid?

There's more—this will blow your mind. Do you vote Republican or Democrat?

None of your business.

No matter. What do you reckon the chances are of America ever electing a black president?

Slim and none.

Well, prepare to be surprised. In 2009, you will send your first black presidential candidate to the White House—not just for one term of office, but two!

My mind is reeling. I can't quite take it in...

You'd better believe it. And it's all a mere thirty or so years down the line for you.

I'll live to see it all?

You will—unless you get run over by a bus.

Ehrlich, the United Nations, the Club of Rome—how did all the experts get it so wrong?

Firstly, their central assumption that world population would continue growing at the same rapid rate will turn out to be flawed. In the years and decades to come, the rate of growth will actually fall—something no one expected.[19] Secondly, as we speak, there's a green agricultural revolution going on that's changing the face of agriculture and boosting food production to levels that will take even the world's best experts by surprise. High-yielding varieties of cereal grains, hybridized seeds, synthetic fertilizers—it's a whole new ballgame.[20]

Never bet against the human race, it would seem.

Not a good idea, no. So you really must stop believing this talk about humanity not being able to feed itself. Any free country with a market economy, half-decent agricultural land, and a willingness to embrace the latest agricultural techniques can feed itself without breaking a sweat. The world has never run out of food, and I don't suspect it ever will.

We could run out of oil and natural resources though, surely?

No, we couldn't.

What makes you so sure?

Common sense. What do you do when you're driving, and your gauge tells you you're low on gas?

I pull over and fill up—duh!

Exactly. You don't go on driving until the tank runs dry, then sit like an idiot at the side of the road wondering what to do next. Society's the same. When any given resource starts to run short—whether it's oil or copper or whatever—we look for more and "fill up."

But what if there isn't any more? I mean, resources are finite.

Then we'll try the next best alternative. The finite resources of the planet are no match for the infinite ingenuity of human beings, and the immutable law of supply and demand.

Whoa! You're getting a bit evangelical there, if you don't mind my saying so.

I guess I am getting carried away, aren't I? But the point is, we've never run out of any natural resource. In the twenty-first century, the world is awash in base metals, precious metals, diamonds, oil, and natural gas. You name it, we've found it. And in the most inaccessible of places. Especially oil.

So you're saying there's no such thing as peak oil?

Look—use your common sense instead of believing everything you read in the media. Do you know how much oil there is on the planet? Does anybody know?

No, I suppose not. All we can be sure of is proven reserves.

Exactly. So when people say we have twenty years of oil left, what they're referring to is the proven reserves—the oil we know is there. As we get closer to that limit, we start to look for more oil so we can "fill up." And guess what? We always find it. Or we find new ways of extracting what's already there.

Your optimism can sometimes be nauseating.

And your pessimism can sometimes be debilitating.

Touché!

The history of the world is the triumph of optimism over pessimism. Are you an investor? Do you have a share portfolio?

A small one, yes.

Why do you invest?

What do you mean, "Why do I invest?" Because I believe my shares will go up over time, that's why.

Despite the constant ups and downs in the market?

Despite the constant ups and downs.

Ha—so you *are* an optimist! You'd have to be; otherwise you'd keep your money under the mattress.

Are you going to give me a share tip?

Maybe later. The point I'm trying to make is that the history of the world is like the stock market—a relentless increase in the general wellbeing of people, despite constant ups and downs.

Prove it.

Why don't you prove it for yourself when I'm gone? Pick any point in our long and distant past. Choose any criterion of progress you like—infant mortality, food output, air quality, treatment of workers or children, levels of democracy, whatever—and compare it to today. You will find a constant and steady improvement over time.

No exceptions?

None that I'm aware of. If you find one, go and tell *The New York Times*, because you'll have made the discovery of the century.

You're looking at your watch. Are you going soon?

I have to. My time is calling. I have a golf game on.

What's life like in the future?

You wouldn't understand it if I told you.

Try me.

Google. Wikipedia. Cellphone. SMS. E-mail. iPad. Cruise missile. Pilotless drone. Hubble telescope. Mars Rover. CD-ROM. DVD. GPS. Gigabyte. PC. Laptop.

GM food. Digital photography. Remote microscopic surgery.

Huh?!

Exactly. It means nothing to you. It's like trying to explain photography to an artist from the Renaissance. But I can tell you about the things that you'll be able to do in my time.

I'm all ears!

You won't need the post office any more—you'll be able to send letters all around the world in a split-second and get a reply just as fast. You'll have all the information you can ever think of available at the touch of a button, from recipes and the daily newspapers to world history. Everyone will have a handheld phone, just like those communicators the crew use in *Star Trek*; you'll be able to call people from anywhere at any time. Your camera will never need a roll of film ever again. You will have music wherever you go. You'll be able to do your shopping from the comfort of your own home. The prices of the most sought-after goods will come down year after year. Everything will become smaller, lighter, and more efficient. Certain kinds of watches will become so cheap that they'll be given away as promotional items. Cars will have automatic guidance systems—you just type in the address of the place you want to go, and it will tell you how to get there. And they've just started testing cars that can drive themselves, and—

Stop! I'm not so sure I want to hear any more.

Isn't it exciting?

It is. But it's unsettling too.

That's because you don't understand it yet. It's the future. And it will unfold in its own time.

What about that share tip you promised?

Ah, yes. Got a pen and paper?

Right here. Go ahead.

Apple.

There's one in the fruit bowl. Help yourself.

No—Apple is a company.

Never heard of it.

> You will, in a couple of years' time. Invest in this company as soon as it lists on the stock exchange.

What on earth will it make—fruit?

> No—personal computers.

Who on earth would want to buy a computer?

> More people than you think. In my time, Apple's market value will exceed the Gross Domestic Product of Greece.[21]

Wow!

> Throw a couple of thousand dollars at the stock, sit on it for thirty years, and you'll retire a millionaire.

The future is suddenly looking very rosy! Thank you.

> You're welcome.

Are there big scares in the twenty-first century too? Is anyone warning of the end of civilisation as we know it?

There is, actually. His name is Al Gore.

What's his story?

Global warming. He thinks we're all going to fry unless we stop pumping fossil fuels into the atmosphere. He's outdone Ehrlich. There's going to be famine, wars, melting ice caps, rising sea levels—it's the whole nine yards.

Global cooling; global warming—can't these alarmists make up their minds?

Oh, I wouldn't worry about it. End-of-the-world scare scenarios are like buses: if you wait long enough, another one soon comes along. In any event, history always makes fools of the prophets of doom.

Bob's Laws on Doomsday Scenarios

1. Doomsday scenarios are by definition flawed, because they are framed in the present and are therefore bound by the limits of knowledge of the present.

2. Doomsday scenarios are never just slightly wrong; they turn out to be hopelessly, utterly, and even comically wrong.

3. Human beings are endlessly inventive. Our capacity to unlock the secrets of the universe is as infinite as the universe itself. So, therefore, is our capacity to solve problems and adapt to changing circumstances.

4. Humanity progresses by moving forward, not backward. Trying to reverse or "disinvent" something that society depends on for its well-being, on the grounds that this might solve a long-term problem, is never the answer.

5. It is often when things are at their worst, and the crisis seems insoluble, that the solution reveals itself—neatly, simply, and to the general surprise of everyone.

This is my long-run forecast in brief.
The material conditions of life will continue to get better for most people, in most countries, most of the time, indefinitely. Within a century or two, all nations and most of humanity will be at or above today's Western living standards. I also speculate, however, that many people will continue to think and say that the conditions of life are getting worse.[22]

Julian Simon   (1932-1998)

Notes

Chapter 1   The Food Scare

1. Stephen Adams, "Obesity Killing Three Times as Many as Malnutrition," *The Telegraph*, (December 13, 2012).

2. "Thomas Malthus," *Wikipedia*.

3. Ibid.

4. Ibid.

5. "Agriculture," *Wikipedia*.

6. "Thomas Malthus," *Wikipedia*.

7. "Agriculture," *Wikipedia*.

8. "British Agricultural Revolution," *Wikipedia*.

9. Ibid.

Chapter 2   The Coal Scare

1. "William Stanley Jevons," *Wikipedia.*

2. "The Coal Question," *Wikipedia.*

3. Ibid.

4. Ibid.

5. Ibid.

6. Ibid.

7. *Coal – the Timber Crisis,* (Davis: University of California–Davis).

8. Ibid.

9. Ibid.

10. Ibid.

11. Ibid.

12. Gregory Clark and David Jacks, *Coal and the Industrial Revolution, 1700-1869,* (Davis: University of California–Davis), p.2.

13. Ibid., p.25.

14. "Petroleum," *Wikipedia.*

15. "Electricity," *Wikipedia.*

Chapter 3   The Horse-Manure Scare

1. Joel Tarr, "Carriage Horses – History: Urban Pollution – Many Long Years Ago," *American Heritage Magazine,* Carnegie-Mellon University, (October 1971).

2. Ibid.

3. Ibid.

4. Ibid.

5. Ibid.

6. Ibid.

7. Ibid.

8. "From Horse Power to Horsepower," Eric Morris, accessed March 26th, 2012, Horsetalk.co.nz. (Quoting an article by Eric Morris, originally printed in *Access Magazine*, published by the University of California Transportation Centre. Details: uctc.its.berkeley.edu/access/.)

9. "Hopelessly Wrong Predictions", Audience Dialogue, http://www.audiencedialogue.net/predict.html.

10. "From Horse Power to Horsepower," Eric Morris, accessed March 26th, 2012, Horsetalk.co.nz. (Quoting an article by Eric Morris, originally printed in *Access Magazine*, published by the University of California Transportation Centre. Details: uctc.its.berkeley.edu/access/.)

11. Ibid.

12. Ibid.

13. Ibid.

14. Ibid.

15. Ibid.

16. Ibid.

17. "Coney Island and Brooklyn Railroad," *Wikipedia*

18. *History of Public Transportation in New York City*, New York Transit Museum, http://www.transitmuseumeducation.org/trc/background.

19. "From Horse Power to Horsepower," Eric Morris, accessed March 26th, 2012, Horsetalk. co.nz. (Quoting an article by Eric Morris, originally printed in *Access Magazine*, published by the University of California Transportation Centre. Details: uctc.its.berkeley.edu/access/.)

20. "Ford Model T," *Wikipedia*.

21. Ibid.

22. Ibid.

23. Ibid.

24. "Henry Ford," *Wikipedia*.

25. "From Horse Power to Horsepower," Eric Morris, accessed March 26th, 2012, Horsetalk.co.nz. (Quoting an article by Eric Morris, originally printed in *Access Magazine*, published by the University of California Transportation Centre. Details: uctc.its.berkeley.edu/access/.)

26. Ibid.

Chapter 4   The End-of-Civilisation Scare

1. Dan Gardner, *Future Babble: How to Stop Worrying and Love the Unpredictable,* (Virgin Books, 2012), p. 119.

2. Ibid., pp.123-125.

3. "1970s," *Wikipedia*

4. "Global cooling," *Wikipedia*

5. Peter Gwynne, "The Cooling World," *Newsweek*, (April 27, 1975).

6. Ibid.

7. "Paul R. Ehrlich," *Wikipedia*

8. Ibid.

9. Ibid.

10. "The Future's Rubbish," *The Economist*, (November 17, 2011).

11. "Garbage in, garbage out," *The Economist*, (June 3, 1995).

12. John Tierney, "Betting the Planet," *The New York Times*, (December 2, 1990).

13. "The State of Agricultural Commodity Markets," Food and Agriculture Organisation of the United Nations, 2009.

14. Dan Gardner, *Future Babble: How to Stop Worrying and Love the Unpredictable,* (Virgin Books, 2012), p. 231.

15. "Oil Prices: 1946-Present," accessed June 14, 2012, InflationData.com.

16. "Historical Inflation Rate," accessed June 14, 2012, InflationData.com.

17. Dan Gardner, *Future Babble: How to Stop Worrying and Love the Unpredictable,* (Virgin Books, 2012), p. 131.

18. Ibid., p.132.

19. "World Population," *Wikipedia*

20. "Green Revolution," *Wikipedia*

21. "Apple is Now Worth More than Greece," *Yahoo Finance,* (January 25, 2012).

22. Ed Regis, "The Doomslayer," *Wired*, Condé Nast Publications Inc., 2004.

Bibliography

Adams, Stephen. "Obesity Killing Three Times as Many as Malnutrition." *The Telegraph*. December 13, 2012.

Audience Dialogue. "Hopelessly Wrong Predictions." http://www.audiencedialogue.net/predict.html

Bradley, Robert Jr. "The Great Energy Resource Debate (Part II: Neo-Malthusian Alarmism)." *Master Resource*. May 13, 2011.

Chivers, Tom. "Paul Ehrlich Still Prophesying Doom, and Still Wrong." *The Telegraph*. April 26, 2012.

———. "World Population Reaches Seven Billion: Predictions of Doom are Nothing New." *The Telegraph*. October 25, 2011.

Clark, Gregory and David Jacks. *Coal and the Industrial Revolution, 1700-1869.* Davis: University of California–Davis.

Climate Depot. "Fact Sheet on 1970s Coming Ice-Age Claims."

Davies, Stephen. "The Great Horse-Manure Crisis of 1894." *Foundation for Economic Education.* September 1, 2004.

Davis: University of California–Davis. *Coal – the Timber Crisis.*

deMar, Gary. "Environmental Doomsayers Strike Again." *The American Vision.* September 18, 2006.

Food and Agriculture Organisation of the United Nations. "The State of Agricultural Commodity Markets." 2009.

Gardner, Dan. *Future Babble: How to Stop Worrying and Love the Unpredictable.* Virgin Books, 2012.

Gwynne, Peter. "The Cooling World," *Newsweek.* April 27, 1975.

Hadas, Thomas. "7 Billion Reasons Why Malthus Was Wrong." *Reuters*. November 2, 2011.

Heath, Allister. "The World is Richer and Healthier." *The Spectator*. November 30, 2006.

InflationData.com. "Historical Inflation Rate," Accessed June 14, 2012.

———. "Oil Prices: 1946-Present." Accessed June 14, 2012.

Morris, Eric. "From Horse Power to Horsepower." accessed March 26th, 2012, Horsetalk.co.nz.

New York Transit Museum. *History of Public Transportation in New York City*.

Owen, David. *The Conundrum: How Trying to Save the Planet is Making Our Climate Problems Worse.* Short Books, 2012.

Regis, Ed. "The Doomslayer." *Wired*. Condé Nast Publications Inc. 2004.

Ridley, Matt. "Our Fading Footprint for Farming Food." *The Wall Street Journal*. December 21, 2012.

Sutton, Gary. "The Fiction of Climate Science – Why the Climatologists Get It Wrong." *Forbes*. December 4, 2009.

Tarr, Joel. "Carriage Horses – History: Urban Pollution – Many Long Years Ago." *American Heritage Magazine*. Carnegie-Mellon University. October, 1971.

The Economist. "Garbage in, garbage out." June 3, 1995.

———. "Malthus, the False Prophet." May 15, 2008.

———. "The Future's Rubbish." November 17, 2011.

Tierney, John. "Betting the Planet." *The New York Times*. December 2, 1990.

Trewavas, Antony. "Malthus Foiled Again and Again." *Nature*. August 8, 2002.

Wikipedia. "Agriculture."

———. "British Agricultural Revolution."

———. "Coney Island and Brooklyn Railroad."

———. "Electricity."

———. "Ford Model T."

———. "Global cooling."

———. "Green Revolution."

———. "Henry Ford."

——— . "History of Rapid Transit."

———. "Paul R. Ehrlich."

———. "Petroleum."

———. "The Club of Rome."

———. "The Coal Question."

———. "The Population Bomb."

———. "Thomas Malthus."

———. "William Stanley Jevons."

————. "World Population."

Yahoo Finance. "Apple is Now Worth More Than Greece." January 25, 2012.

www.ingramcontent.com/pod-product-compliance
Lightning Source LLC
Chambersburg PA
CBHW021958170526
45157CB00003B/1049